NEW
TESTAMENT
LIVING

Norman B. Harrison, D.D.

New Testament Living
has been reprinted
by
Grace Unshackled
*A ministry dedicated to teaching
the finished work of Christ.*

Minor editing changes
have been made to the original
booklet for reprint and
formatting requirements.

This booklet is available at:
www.leelefebre.com
www.thelifebookstore.com
www.amazon.com

*The book was originally
made available in* 1953

ISBN 9781495985959
ISBN 1495985954

New Testament Living

The Inwardness of the Christian Life

(Thirteen Studies)

Dear

_____

Seldom do we have opportunity to take a course in Christian Living, to learn the distinctive nature of the Christian life and how it is to be lived. May these studies prove themselves most valuable to you, and through you to others.

Sincerely yours,

_____

STUDY ONE

The Abiding Life
The New Secret

Embodied in this phrase, "The Abiding Life," is Jesus' most essential teaching concerning the nature and secret of Christian living—a new and living way.

The Great Transition. For three and a half wonderful years Jesus the Christ, the Lord from heaven, had walked and talked with men, especially with those He had chosen as intimate associates. Now comes the end. His death, resurrection and return to Glory will leave them alone and sad. Not so! "I will not leave you orphans: I will come unto you." And He declares that this will be of real advantage to them: no longer a presence without, merely associating with, but a presence within them, personal to them. They are to have, together with His own promised presence, a great indwelling Teacher, the Holy Spirit: "He will guide you into all the truth."

A New Heart-Language. With this transition is developed a new terminology to fit the new situation. So often those who believed in Him had been designated "disciples": this term is never used in the Epistles. During His lifetime men had been called to "follow" Jesus: they cannot follow Him now. Rather, believers are called to something more intimate and satisfying—an "in" relationship.

He said, "Come unto Me"; but now He says, "Abide in Me." And that little word "in" becomes the most significant, the most dominant word in New Testament language. It is used by Jesus 31 times in John 14 and 15; by Paul 111 times (ARV) in his Ephesians letter.

The New Relationship. To render it realistic Jesus turns to nature for an object lesson—he vine and its branches. The pictured truth is inescapable. The "in" is seen to be "in union with." Christ and His own are joined inwardly as intimately as the vine and its branches. Three lessons are obvious. It is (1) An inner relationship, dependent upon nothing external. (2) A vital relationship, for flow of life from one to the other. (3) An essential relationship: "Apart from Me—severed from Me, separately from Me—ye can do nothing." Nothing? How utterly essential is it to "abide in"!

The New Position—"In Me." Becoming a Christian is not a matter of behavior but of position. Going back to Adam, man was created "in"—in a sacred enclosure with God. Man sinned. "So He drove out the man." Since then every man is born "out." Only by a new, second birth does he come to be "in"—back in fellowship with God, in His fold and favor. By nature every man is "in Adam." He is descended from Adam, shares his nature and lot, his sinfulness and condemnation: that's the way God must deal with him, not according to his individual character or conduct. By a second birth, under the New Covenant, God sees him "in Christ" and treats him as such. He belongs to a new order, a new family, a new race.

The New Possession—"I in You." How startling! Christ really lives in a human being? Yes, "As many as received Him, to them gave He the right to become the children of God," actually "born of God." Just what does it mean to receive Him? Listen to His own explanation: "Behold, I stand at the door and knock: if any man hears My voice, and opens the door"—the door to his inner self—"I will come in to him." He knocked for admittance. Thus clearly the glorified Christ states His purpose to live in the human heart.

Should He fail to gain entrance; should He be kept standing and knocking as Holman Hunt has painted Him—such refusal to receive Him robs the soul within of His saving work. In becoming a Christian you heard His knock and you received Him, just as you would receive a visitor into your home. He came in. He's been "in" you, a part of your person, a priceless possession, ever since. You can say with Paul, and should say over and over to yourself, "Christ lives in me."

The New Provision. Christ is in the Christian, not as an ornament but as the source of new life; yes, and the resource for living this new life. The branch draws all this life from the vine; so must we abide in Him, thus to draw upon Him for life, for the qualities of life which are in Him. Often a man is heard to say, "I'm trying to live a Christian life," which means that he is depending upon himself to do it. His resource is himself. With many others in our churches today he is substituting a good life for a Christian life. He has missed the Vine-and-branch relationship. One must always ask, "Am I living my life? Or is Christ living His life through me?"

A New Product—"Fruit" with the flavor of the Vine. A Christian is set to reproduce, to perpetuate, to propagate the life of Christ. This is possible, not by imitation but by implantation. Years ago God lived with a man. The result was the beautiful, matchless life of Jesus Christ. Today He lives again this time in a man—in you, in me—for this distinct purpose, to demonstrate in human flesh His beauty and His loveliness. How we miss the point!

In utmost devotion one might be heard to say, "I want to give Him my very best." Such a response isn't in the vine-branch picture. Christ doesn't want your best; He expects His best through you. Learn so to abide that there results an unhindered flow of His life through you. Thus your life will come to be Christ-flavored.

A Mutual Interdependence, "You in Me; I in you." The teaching is plain. He is telling us that as branches we have no life in ourselves; we are com-

dependent upon Him for the supply of life. It is all in Him; we must abide in Him and draw it from Him. But—and this amazes us—He is just as completely dependent upon us. Grapes do not grow on the vine; they are always on the branches. If He is to have any fruit it must be through us. He has made Himself completely dependent upon us for the expression of His life. What condescension on His part; what responsibility on our part! Can we offer Him other than Christ-flavored lives!

An Effortless Life. How slowly do we arrive at this simple fact, that true New Testament living is effortless. The branch does not try to produce fruit, any more than the electric light bulb tries to shine. Confessedly neither has any need to try; they simply draw upon their inexhaustible supply of life and energy. In doing so they scarcely touch the fringe of their resources. Yet the Christian has infinitely greater resources; the One who created vegetable life and electric energy—that One lives in us. Why do we need to try? Only because we are not abiding. Then the truest test of Christian living is in the question: Am I trying? Or am I abiding? If I find myself still trying I am not as yet an unchoked channel through which His life may flow.

Editor's Note: *At the end of each study, we have placed a list of the Scripture addresses that Mr. Harrison used in that chapter's study. The verses and passages are noted in the order of their use and referral in the text.*

The list below applies to Study One.

John 14:18; 16:13 RV; Matt 11:28
John 15:4; Gen 2:8; 3:24; John 1:12, 13;
Rev. 3:20; Gal. 2:20; John 15:5
John 15:8; 15:4

STUDY TWO

The Inner Life
Not Religion—But a Life

The Failure of Religion. The word religion occurs but four times in the entire Bible. We trace it back to the Latin *religio*, meaning to bind or obligate. It conveys the sense of duty. Its realm is the outward: religious ceremony, service, conduct. In the Bible it is chiefly synonymous with Judaism, degraded to a religion in Christ's day. It was religion that put Christ on the Cross. The world's religions all fail in this: they have no divine person capable of imparting life. The word religion seemingly never escaped the lips of Jesus. He did not come to found a religion but to bring <u>life</u>. Religion is man striving after God. Jesus brought God to man, and man to God.

The Gift of Life. "I came that they may have life, and may have it abundantly." "I give unto them eternal life." The word "life" occurs some forty times in John's Gospel alone, and the writer concludes the gospel with this statement of purpose: "These are written that you may believe that Jesus is the Christ, the Son of God: and that believing you may have life in His name." Life is inward. This eternal life is Christ's gift of His own life.

And how, may we ask, is physical life acquired? Science knows of but one way of imparting life—by birth. Hence Jesus presented the new birth as the one great imperative. Spiritual life comes only through spiritual birth.

Jesus' Purpose in the Sermon on the Mount is to sweep away religious profession and pretense and bring men back to the realities of the inner heart-life. (1) Note those He counts blessed: the pure in heart. (2) For entrance into His kingdom He requires a righteousness beyond religious externalism, beyond man's best efforts. (3) He has come to install a new heart-standard. "You have heard that it was said to them of old time, Thou shalt not kill." Restrain yourself from killing and you've kept the law; but here is Christ's New Testament standard: "But I say unto you, if you have anything in your heart that would prompt the act, in the sight of God it is as though you had done it."

The old standard forbids the act of adultery. Jesus brushes that aside with His new demand: there must be nothing in the heart that would prompt the act. Does Jesus ask that you love just your neighbor and those who love you? No, indeed! Love even your enemy! Jesus demands a very high heart-standard, and He came to create a new heart within us capable of meeting His high ideal.

Keeping the Commandments. If we respond to the Ten Commandments with the prescribed kind of conduct, do this or don't do that, have we kept them? Jesus said: No, that is simply religious formality. Rather, He said, the first commandment is Love (the Lord God); the second is like it, love (your neighbor). Without the heart conditional conduct is mere behaviorism; it fails to meet the requirement. "Love is the fulfilling of the law." What a rebuke to the legalistic religionists of His day! And of our day!

Religious Hypocrites. Repeatedly Jesus clashed with the religionists of His day, till they finally put Him on the Cross. In Matthew 23 He had an inning with them: "Woe unto you, scribes and Pharisees, hypocrites! For you cleanse the outside of the cup and of the platter, but within they are full from extortion and excess."

What is a hypocrite? An actor, one who plays a part, seeking to appear what he is not, using religious behavior to cover up what he really is.

And men fall for that! "Man looks on the outward appearance, but God looks on the heart." Jesus' teaching exposed the rottenness of the human heart; He will have "truth in the inward parts." Jesus, brushing aside human sham, offered to the race His life, pure, holy, heart-cleansing, as the fountainhead of all true living.

"Not under Law, but under Grace." Law and religion are in the same class: they deal with externals; hence they tend to hypocrisy, to a covering up of the real heart condition. One can act up to the Law's requirements without being up to them. How many hypocrites have we in our churches, ignorant of the life under grace? Yes, and using grace for license?

What does grace do? Grace brought God from Glory to live in a human body. In that body He died to bring men to Himself, rose again and ascended to heaven. Now, by the same grace He will, as a life—giving Spirit, come and live in any body—in anyone who will receive Him. What grace! By His inliving presence He cleanses the heart, so there is nothing to conceal, and the life becomes "sincere," that is transparent, "clear to the light." Doing away with sham.

Galatianism. We cannot thank God enough for the Galatian error, occasioning the book that delivers from behaviorism and externalism—do this and do that to commend yourself to God. Paul met this by saying, "If you do, Christ will profit you nothing; you are fallen away from grace" as a life-principle; that is, you have gone back to the law system of living, back to external regulating of your life. But if you as a Christian are really living under grace, you do not need to try to live a good life. Take for example the matter of honesty. You do not need to try to be honest. Rather you should draw upon Christ living in you—He is 100% honest. His proposal to pour His honesty through you is a perfect guarantee of honesty! You do not need to try to be pure; you will be pure as you draw upon His perfect purity. Abiding is the answer.

Christ Formed Within. Christ taught us of His inliving presence; but it remained for Paul, faced with this Galatian hypocrisy, to urge the proving of its practical value. Eager to have the Christ-life realized in his beloved converts, he cries with heart-yearning, as of a woman with child: "My little children, of whom I am again in travail until Christ be formed in you." Formed! As the fountain of all thinking, loving, willing, planning and daily living. Here then is the challenge: that as the Virgin Mary yielded her body to the Holy Spirit to give the Lord Jesus a flesh and blood existence and expression, just so we turn our bodies over to the Spirit, that He may form Christ in us and thus we in turn give Him a flesh and blood existence and expression in our day—even through us.

John 10:10, 28, 20:31; 3:3, 7; Matt. 5:21

I Sam: 16:7; Ps. 51:6; Rom. 6:14;

Phil. 1:10; Gal. 5:2, 4; Gal. 4:19

Matt. 5;22, 27, 28 43, 44; Matt. 22:36-40; 23:25

STUDY THREE

Philosophy of the Christian Life
Romans Truth

Romans the Essential Book. Romans is the must book of the Bible, not merely because it sets forth the basic doctrine of the Christian faith but, back of the doctrine, the true philosophy of life. The philosophy is the key to God's dealings with men; hence everyone should have a grasp of Romans. Briefly: God has given the race two federal heads—Adam and Christ (called the last Adam). God treats all men as in one or the other. By natural birth all men are "in Adam." All are descended from him, derive their life from him, are associated with him, have their standing in him. Only by a second, spiritual birth does anyone come to be "in Christ" with standing in Him.

IN Spells I-dentificatio-N. We here visualize this for our help in grasping Romans 1 to 8.

> **In Adam**—All Identified with Adam (1:1-3;20) in Sin, Condemnation and Death
>
> **In Christ**—He Identified with us in Flesh and Blood (3:21-5-21)
>
> We Identified with Him in Death and Resurrection (6)
>
> He Identified with Us in Living Presence (8)

Adam Ruined the Race—1:1-3:20. By virtue of his headship Adam, when he sinned, took the whole human race with him—away from God. Man is out away from his Creator. Read his resulting degradation, Rom. 1:18-32. This explains the moral breakdown of mankind, more evident today than ever. There is nothing man can do to undo his identification with God. "We have before proved both Jews and Gentiles, that they are all under sin." The Old Testament asserts man's total ruin: "There is none righteous, no, not one." By the law of inheritance man's speech and behavior betray his descent from Adam. So the case against man sums up thus: "That every mouth may be stopped, and all the world may become guilty before God." The reason every man needs to be saved is simply that he has been born into a race that a righteous God must condemn in toto.

God's Remedy: He Becomes a Man—3:21-5:21. To provide a second federal head God identified Himself with us, taking our flesh and blood. Consider what this involved. He became a part of the race He had already condemned—how amazing! He came to share our lot. Since "the wages of sin is death" He will take that death. (He was born to die, Heb. 2:14.) There He is on the Cross, taking our place, receiving what we deserved.

And note this: there had to be a God in heaven to condemn God on the Cross, one who could judicially transfer our guilt to Him. By that blood, that sinless, poured-out life we become justified. Yes, and by grace. What is grace? God taking upon Himself what we deserved, thus freeing Himself to give us what we did not deserve. Then we are justified by faith. All have a bad record with God, as exemplified by Abraham and David—Romans 4. Christ takes that bad record Himself and reckons to us His own perfect record, if we simply believe.

"By One Man": Adam or Christ—5:12-21. "By one man sin entered into the world, and death by sin; and so death passed upon all men." By the righteousness of one the free gift came upon all men to justification of life." Through "one" to "all"—this is the philosophy of God's dealings with men. There can be no exception. (Everyone should read this remarkable summing up of the case.)

We Share in Christ's Death and Resurrection—Romans 6. Christians are described as "we who died to sin." When did we die? The answer is: When Christ died. "Don't you know"—v.30. We are to "know" as a basic, accomplished fact that we are identified with Christ in His death, burial and resurrection, thus to "walk in newness of life."

What makes this possible? "Knowing that our old man—the sinful self we inherited from Adam—was crucified jointly, with Christ." He took our flesh and blood that He might nail it in deserved death to the Cross; it is just as though we ourselves had hung there. But what kind of a death and life? A death to sin, leading out into a life unto God. So-"likewise reckon ye also yourselves to be dead indeed unto sin, but alive unto God through Jesus Christ our Lord." Do not struggle to make it so; reckon it is so.

If you are a Christian, God sees you to have died with Christ and been raised with Him.

See yourself as He sees you, and go out to live thus: "Yield yourselves unto God as those who are alive from the dead." It is a new way of living: "not under law"—making yourself behave—"but under grace"—grace that rendered you "dead to the law by the body of Christ; that you should be married to Another." The living Christ. How very wonderful! Identified with Him in death to be joined to Him in life.

He identifies Himself with Us in Living Presence—Romans 8. "Now in Christ"-this new position which is ours, in union with Him—"there is no condemnation" as there was in Adam. Instead, "The law," meaning the inward control or power, "of the Spirit of life in Christ Jesus has made me free from the law (control) of sin and death." I have a new resource, a living presence within. Something has happened to me! And I make this deliverance practically mine as I "walk not after the flesh"—my inheritance from Adam—"but after the Spirit"—my resource in Christ. And now—"since Christ is in us"—we are under no obligation whatever to live after the promptings of the flesh. A glorious release!

Too Good to Be True! In Adam we were utterly condemned. There was not a ray of hope for any of us. But now, because we are in Christ He says to us, "I'll come and live in you." Whoever heard of such a transformation, such an utterly changed situation! We have now entered into the farewell teaching of Jesus: "Abide in Me"—that's Romans 8:1; "and I in you"—that's Romans 8:10. Now He is our resource, and "we are more than conquerors." No circumstance can defeat us, drawing upon His patience, purity, love and power in inexhaustible supply. Praise to His Name!

Rom. 3:9, 10, 19; 6:23; Isa. 53:6; Rom. 4:1-8;
Rom. 5:12, 18; Rom 6:1-4, 6-11
Rom. 6:13; 7:4: 8:1, 2, 10, 12, 37

STUDY FOUR

God Sees Three Men

Corinthians Truth

In the popular mind men are loosely grouped as Christian and non-Christian, presumably saved and unsaved. But this is superficial, even deceptive. In fact, many are self-deceived, counting themselves Christians when they are not. Man's rating of himself is wholly indeterminate. God alone is the judge.

God's Threefold Classification. Racially, by natural birth, every man is a Jew or a Gentile. By a second, spiritual birth any Jew, any Gentile may become a member of the Church of God. This division is clear-cut, with no overlapping. But our concern in this study is with a grouping still more intimate and personal. Viewing humanity God sees three men, only three: the Natural Man; the Carnal Man; the Spiritual Man. Every man is given his true rating, his standing or lack of standing with God. Since you must be one of the three, you should face the question: Which am I?

The Natural Man. His portrait is drawn in one significant sentence (read it carefully—I Cor. 2:14.) Who is he? The man as he came from his parents, may be richly endowed; well-mannered, even highly educated; a fine product of society. But he is untouched by the Spirit of God. The Spanish Bible reads, "the animal man." In common with the animal world he caters to his creature comforts.

He is spiritually incapacitated, a stranger to the things of the Spirit, "neither can he know them, because they are spiritually discerned." Reading the Bible he cannot take it in. Thus Jesus berated men of His day: having eyes they saw not, having ears they heard not. Sad! The only remedy is a new birth. To one born of the Spirit God gives a spiritual eye, a spiritual ear back of the physical. How much the natural man misses. "Ye must be born again" just to enjoy the here and now.

The Spiritual Man. "But he that is spiritual."

Who is he? One born of the Sprit, assuredly. But more: he is controlled by the Spirit, characterized by the Spirit, walks in the Spirit, confronts His fellows with the fruit of the Spirit. And to reveal the secret of such it is said, "We have the mind of Christ." How is that mind acquired? By birth. Just as the babe born into the human family possesses potentially the mind of a man, so one born into the divine family is endowed with the mind of Christ. What possibilities! The life expressive of the mind of Christ will take on His loveliness of character.

Paul's Problem Church. Confessedly one born of the Spirit should at once go on to be Spirit-controlled and Spirit-characterized.

What might not the Church of Christ be and do, were this the case! But, sad to say, it is not. The majority of Christians are content to be "saved." Only half-made, half-saved, so to speak, they are still dominated by the flesh. Such was the Corinthian church, characterized by divisions, lawsuits, divorces, immoralities of various sorts. These conditions occasioned the Corinthian letters. This fleshly man, who ought not to be, who wrecks the church today as he did at Corinth—this man is our chief concern in this study.

The Carnal Man. "I could not speak unto you as unto spiritual, but as unto carnal." An abnormality! He is a man born of the Spirit but continuing to be controlled, yes, dominated by the flesh. (Carnal is the adjective form of flesh.) Three characteristics are cited: (1) As to spiritual growth, mere babes—a case of arrested growth, of protracted babyhood. How many, babylike, can't walk or talk? (2) As to diet, "I fed you with milk, not with meat." Capable of taking only baby food they will never arrive at maturity. (3) As to conduct, "envying, strife, divisions" being among them, they "walk as men," that is, just like unsaved men. They are retaining the traits of the natural man.

Facing the Final Test. Christian character is likened to a building with Christ the foundation. A building must conform to its foundation; hence the immense responsibility to maintain a level of Christ-conformed living. It makes New Testament standards exceedingly searching. "If any man build upon this foundation gold, silver, precious stones" (qualities of the spiritual man), "wood, hay, stubble" (worthless materials of the carnal man), the final fire-test that is coming will reveal the true nature of the life that has been lived.

So Paul warns the carnal folks in the Corinthian church—his problem church with its shameful out-croppings of the flesh. Such wood-hay-stubble living is but fuel for the fire. Query: How many Corinthian churches and Christians have we today?

Glorious Gain or Utter Loss. Poles apart are these two. The spiritual and the carnal man. The one having lived in the Sprit, his works shall "abide"; "he shall receive a reward." (A subject worthy of study.) Added to the gift of eternal life, the gracious principle of rewards amazes us, offered as an incentive to live wholly on the spiritual level.

The other man faces unutterable loss. His salvation was settled at the Cross, dependent on nothing he had done or could do; yet his carnality leaves him stripped of his life-works. Unsuited to Glory, they (his life-works) must perish in the fire. What warning this!

The Corrective Consideration: the Indwelling Presence. Just one climactic reminder—this reproof: "Don't you know that you are the temple of God, and that the Sprit of God dwells in you?" Add this further reproof: "What? Don't you know that your body is a temple of the Holy Spirit which is in you?" The great fact about you is that God lives in you. How dare you dishonor Him? Consider then: there is no spot on earth more sacred than your body. God made it, and chose it to live in—all for His glory. What a challenge to holy living!

Make the Adjustment. You can never be the same; you have taken another Person into your life. Were he merely an ordinary person you would adjust your living to his presence; how much more to the highest and best. Adjust all your thinking, loving , planning, purposing to His pleasure. Living will take on new meaning, a new delightfulness, a new ease of expression.

Make the Holy Spirit at Home. He has left heaven, choosing your heart instead as His home. Are you affronting Him with anything distasteful to Him? Anything that grieves Him, makes Him uncomfortable? Rather, give Him the run of the house— make Him at home in every room. Make this your test of New Testament living—God and you homing together. Habitually thank Him: "Thank You, Holy Spirit, for coming to live in me."

I Cor. 10:32; 2:14, 15; John 3:7; I Cor. 2:16;
I Cor. 3:1-3, 9-13; I Cor. 3:13, 15, 16; 6:19

STUDY FIVE

Saved by Grace—Live in Grace
Galatians Truth

The average man, saved by grace, has yet to demonstrate the richness of the life in the resources of grace.

An Entirely Different Way of Life. We came into the Christian life through the doorway of grace. "By grace are ye saved through faith...not of yourselves.... not of works, lest any man should boast." Salvation is not of works, deeds such as law or religion require of us. The contrast is clear-cut. Grace is God setting aside what man seeks to do of and for himself. God does it; and under grace God continues to do it.

Two Distinct Realms. Romans makes this a

fact doubly emphatic. "Ye are not under the law, but under grace." Read the entire statement; it confronts us with the failure of living under law. Law has no delivering power. To be delivered from sin we must live in this new realm. "Ye are become dead to the law (as a way of living) by the body of Christ; that ye should be married to another"—the living Christ becomes the center and inspiration of a new mode of life. Yet man has such an overwhelming confidence in himself that he is as prone to return to his old way of living as the compass needle is to fly back to the north.

The Galatian Issue. Teachers, propagandists for Judaism and zealous for law observance, had come among Paul's converts. Paul promptly stigmatized their preachments "another gospel" that invites the anathema of God. Strong language surely, but mixing of law and grace is an offense to God; it must be dealt a body-blow. (Yet it persists today.) "Christ has redeemed us from the curse of the law." Shall we go back to a system from which we were redeemed, bought out from under, at such great cost? Thank God for the Galatian letter.

The Failure of Law. Law is an expedient for regulating conduct. But consider: You cannot make a law that will compel a man to keep it. We have law against stealing; so presumably, nobody steals! Against murder; so nobody murders? Nonsense! More: what if man does not want to keep the law? Still more: what if he is incapable of keeping it? Such is the case. Man is a sinner, by his first birth, incapable of measuring up to God's law. Thus the law system is largely limited to a negative purpose: "By the law is the knowledge of sin."

Law a Temporary System. Law's paramount failure lies in its inability to meet man's fundamental need—his need of life. Here it is impotent. Written over it is the time limit word "until." The law was only until God's time for ushering in His perfect plan in Christ the Life-Giver. Grace brought Him all the way from Glory to give His life for us, that now, the barrier of sin removed, He might give His life to us. And how does He give us His life? Only by giving us Himself: "He that has the Son has life; he that has not the Son of God has not life." Amazing grace! Is it possible that you or I would ever revert to the old way of living?

The Two Systems Contrasted. Law is man doing something for God. Grace is God doing something for man. Law is a man-centered system of living, a life of dependence upon self and self-effort. Grace is a Christ-centered system of living, a life of dependence upon Him and His inexhaustible resources. Under law a man is his own sole resource; it summons him to be good, and do good. He must depend wholly upon himself—do the best he can. It is strange, but this appeals to man's self-confidence; failing, he is ever ready to try again. But to live in grace—what a sweet sense of release!

The Resources of Grace. In setting aside the law with its appeal to men to behave thus and so, Galatians presents the two matchless resources of grace, which determine the character of New Testament living and guarantee its success.

(1) Christ's Indwelling. "Christ lives in me." If true, this is the most startling fact in human experience. Nothing could approach it The One who created all things and now holds them together (Col. 1:17)—a most meaningful statement in this atomic age—that Person lives in me! In you! How amazing! How astounding! Goodbye behaviorism. Something has happened to you and only resultantly to your conduct. You are a different person. Christ is your supernatural resource for life's living. What is more, you have a new incentive in life; it has taken on new purpose and meaning. You want, above all else, to please Him. What a privilege to let Him live out His life through you!

(2) The Holy Spirit's Inworking. Under grace the Spirit has been given to me specifically to end my minority, my law-controlled days. I no longer live under rules and regulations. Now, with Sprit's inward control, the Father can treat me as His son, a grown-up He can trust. The Spirit, working in me a loyalty to which I was a stranger, begets a life of constant peace, joy and triumph.

The situation may be visualized thus:

> **Law** — Appeals to me; I am my sole resource.
>
> **Grace** — Supplies the resource of the inliving Christ and inworking Spirit.

What Is Falling from Grace? Law and grace are opposing principles by which to live. Falling from grace, failing to avail yourself of its resources (as above), there is but one thing to fall to—Law. You go back to your former way of living; you depend upon yourself and your good (?) behavior; you do the best, or the worst, that you can. The Word says, "Christ shall profit you nothing." Of course not; you are depending not upon Him but upon yourself. What results? You may revert to drunkenness, if that is in your background. It may be anger, worry or impatience—anything in the potential of your make-up, since you are no longer abiding.

What is Living in Grace? To live in grace is to draw, constantly, momentarily, upon the implanted resources of grace. It is to have complete confidence in the inliving Christ, that He is both willing and able to control every phase of life.

It is to pass from Romans 7—with its I-try, I-fail, I'm-discouraged life, into Romans 8—with its In-Christ life; its Christ-in-me life; its Spirit-prompted, Spirit-guided life; its all-things-working-together-for-good life; its more-than-conqueror life; its inseparable-and-undefeatable life. To live in grace is daily to prove that the grace that saved us is all-sufficient for every need and every circumstance.

Eph. 2:8, 9; Rom. 6:14, 7:4; Gal. 1:6-9, 3:13
Rom. 3:20; Gal 3;21, 22; John 10:10; I John 5:12
Gal. 2:20; II Cor. 5:9 RV, 5:15; Gal. 4:6, 7
Gal. 5:4, 2; Rom. 8:28-39

STUDY SIX

Christ Is The Only Answer

Ephesians Truth

Our Thesis in this study is that we fall short of New Testament living so long as we fail to live the Ephesians way; that we are still in the realm of behaviorism until we live inwardly controlled by our Head. (Keep in mind the progressive unfolding of truth. Ephesians is a new high.)

Paul's Favorite Figure. Running throughout Paul's church epistles is the conception of the Church as the Body of Christ; that the Church is essentially an *organism* back of all organization. This embodies Jesus' teaching of the inwardness of our relationship to Him—vine-and-branch abiding; but it carries further. Union secures unity. (This makes room for diversity, as in Romans; but leaves no room for divisions, as in Corinthians.) We are in the realm of personality. The body gives expression to the inner life action: the body responds to the mind and will of the head.

For the Glory of God. "The chief end of man is to glorify God" (Shorter Catechism). But unredeemed man does not do it, yes, cannot do it; hence the glory of God is redemption's essential goal. The Father chose us in Christ. Why? "That we should be unto the praise of His glory." Then the Spirit sealed us to Himself. Why? That we should be "unto the praise of His glory." Thus redemption terminates, not upon us but upon God. It means this: the entire Godhead, the Father, the Son and the Spirit are entrusting their reputation to you and me. Jesus' life-work was glorifying His Father (John 17:4). He has handed us the torch.

This is our life-work—nothing less. Why? We may ask. Because we are both the New Testament temple and body of Christ in which to reproduce His life on earth. When the tabernacle was finished "the glory of God filled the house." So also the temple. Then Christ came, "and tabernacled among us, and we beheld His glory." Having finished His work

He turned His glory over to us, saying to the Father, "The glory Thou gave Me I have given them." Wonderful! His glory in trust! "What? Know ye not that your body is the temple of the Holy Spirit which is in you, which ye have of God, and ye are not your own? For ye are bought with a price: therefore glorify God in your body."

Called thus to portray the beauty and loveliness of our God through these human personalities, how dare we, by an act of ill-will, self-will, impatience, or anything of the sort obscure the glory of His presence within? Far from representing Him, we so miserably misrepresent Him. But how can we ever attain to so lofty a standard? To that question Ephesians is the answer.

The Body Is The "Fullness" Of The Head. In the most majestic language we are reminded how God raised up Christ, set Him at His right hand, in a position above all authority, and "appointed Him universal and supreme Head of the Church, which is His Body, the completeness of Him who everywhere fills the universe with Himself" (Weymouth). What honor! The most wonderful person in the world, and we have become His fullness or completeness! Exactly so. The head finds its fullness of expression through the body.

Here we find the same interdependence as was noted in the vine-and-branch relationship. While the body depends on the head for its wisdom and direction, since it has none of its own, the head depends on the body for the expression of its mind, its will, its wisdom. Thus the inner relationship of John 15 (read vv. 1-5) becomes an inwardly controlled partnership, each doing its appointed part, for the perfecting of this new personality, the "new man."

Out of Control. Now we are confronted with a portrait of ourselves and how we behaved in utter disregard of God. "Dead in trespasses and sins" means we were dead to God; they controlled us, God did not. We walked according to the world, the flesh and the devil; they swayed us; they mastered us; they had their way with us. Read Ephesians 2:1-3. These three verses picture our utterly hopeless condition, "by nature children of wrath." Out of God's control.

Redemption's Problem. This condition of man clearly reveals the nature of the problem redemption is set to solve. Go back to Genesis, back to sin's inception. What happened in the Garden of Eden?

Satan had a subtle plan. He drove a wedge between God and man; he ruined the "control" God had created in man; he rendered man unresponsive to God; he took man out from under the authority of God. It is this damage Christ has come to repair. Not to make men good, but to bring man back under divine control. He must regain His inner control. This He does as the Head.

Could the law meet this need? Never. Any control it exercises is from without; hence its failure as a system of life. So law was God's temporary measure "until"—until Christ came to be "the end of the law" with His perfect plan of control from within.

Effective Union With Christ. God had a plan fully equal to the situation. In His grace Christ did not die and rise alone; He "made us alive together with" Him; has already seated us in Christ in the heavenlies; and He purposes to pour out His kindness upon us through eternity. (Here read and rejoice over Eph. 2:6, 7.)

What marvelous grace! But not its effectiveness. We are His new creation, responsive to Him: "created in Christ Jesus for good works"—not just any good works, but the particular good works "which God afore prepared that we should walk in them." We used to walk responsive to the world, the flesh and the devil (vv. 2, 3). What assurance has He that we will now walk as He would have us? What has happened? Christ is our Head, to control our walk as completely as the head controls our feet. This is nothing short of wonderful! Do you live this way?

"One New Man, So making Peace." Effective for the individual, this plan is equally for groups and classes of society. God's one solution for their enmity is the Cross, having slain the enmity thereby. His plan is to build all factions into "one body," He Himself in control as the Head. Envision how completely this would remedy the world's ills. But man will not have God's peace plan. He will not have Him who "is our peace." Hence the world must have war. A warring world is traceable to a rejected Cross.

More Than A Body—A Building. As the human body has back of the flesh a structure for housing a person, we "are builded together for an habitation of God through the Spirit." Paul's ministry was to build this New Testament temple. And now in a dedicatory prayer He invokes the inliving presence of the Godhead: the Holy Spirit strengthening you inwardly, Christ dwelling in your heart by faith, God filling you to the utmost, that there may be "glory in the church" as in the tabernacle and temple of old. What a climax! We began with the glory of God entrusted to His redeemed. In these wonderful chapters we have seen God's plan for securing that glory through the church. As it shone out through Christ, so now through His mystical body. What a culmination! We are back under His authority, controlled by His glory!

The Walk Expresses the Head. Naturally the duty enjoined by Ephesians is to "walk." Walking expresses the person. But how do one's feet walk? In complete control of the head. They have no problem of conduct. Instinctively, unhesitatingly, they behave according to the head. This is New Testament living. It has one simple condition. Let your foot represent you having become a member of the body of Christ. Portraying you it has personality, hence a mind and a will. Suppose it insists upon retaining its own mind and will. You would be frustrated in every move. It's time to get up; but Mr. Foot says, "No, I'm not ready." You must be off to work; but Mr Foot protests, "I don't feel like it today".

What a predicament! Does Christ have to face such frustration in His Body? The lesson is inescapable. The primal condition for New Testament living is yieldedness. Yes, and with the yielding must be abiding. Only as the foot and hand, through sinews, blood vessels and nerves, abide in the head can they be yielded to the head. So we, abiding and yielding, live in Christ, draw upon Christ, respond to Christ—nothing short of this is true New Testament living.

A New Purpose In Life. What is your body for? Simply to please your head. All its movements and functions are devoted to this one end. And we are a Body with such a wonderful Head to please. All life's complexity is reduced to utter simplicity! Living thus you are under His sweet, loving, complete control. Why live any other way? "Henceforth, Lord Christ my Head, let Thy mind and will be my control."

Eph. 1:3-14, 6; Eph. 1:6, 12, 14; Ex 40:33-35;
II Chron. 7:1; John 1:14; 17:22; I Cor. 6:19, 20;
Eph. 1:22, 23; 2:1-3; Gen 3:1-13; Rom. 10:4;
Eph. 2:4-7, 10, 13-18, 22; 3:16-21; 4;1, 17; 5; 1, 2, 8

STUDY SEVEN

The "Unselfed" Life
Philippians Truth

The Philippians Problem. A delightful problem it is. Paul is in prison at Rome. Ten years before, unjustly imprisoned at Philippi, he and Silas were singing praises at midnight. Now from the Roman prison comes this letter saturated with the spirit of praise. Its key verse is "Rejoice in the Lord always; and again I say, Rejoice." Constantly it calls upon Christians to "joy and rejoice." Evidently Paul's mind and spirit are not in prison. What an unheard-of reaction to finding one's self in jail! How can we explain it? Simply stated: the overtone of Philippians is Rejoice, only because its undertone is an "Unselfed" Life.

To Me To Live Is ____?____. Just how would we, in honesty, complete the declaration of life-interest? Business? Family? Studies? Career? With Paul Christ was enthroned. He has one concern: that "Christ shall be magnified in my body, whether by life or by death." Such a life knows no defeat; it is always on top.

With most of us our inner spirit is sadly sensitive to our outer circumstance. Our spirit is small, shriveled by self-interest. Six times in this chapter Paul shows concern for "the gospel." There is the secret! Be occupied with something bigger than yourself. Paul is joyously free in a no-concern for self.

Paul's Spiritual Secret. Paul was a sufferer. We believe God used his "thorn in the flesh" to stabilize his spiritual life. Doubtless it was eye trouble which disfigured his face, rendering him despicable in public—a serious handicap. He prayed three times for its removal. Here is the answer, not on the physical but the high spiritual level; "My grace is sufficient for thee." "Paul you don't need that thorn removed. It shall be a reminder of your dependence upon Me and My all-sufficiency for you."

Paul took this as his answer. "Most gladly,

therefore, will I rather glory in my infirmities, that the power of Christ may rest upon me. Therefore, I take pleasure" in the things most folks gripe and grumble about. (See II Cor. 6:1-10.) This is the making of the man who later says, "None of these things move me." He is inducted into an "unselfed" life.

High Spiritual Values in Suffering. Chapter one ends on the note of suffering. When we need help we naturally turn to David or Paul—both great sufferers. Our Lord Himself "learned obedience by the things which He suffered." Is there any easier way for us? He sits "as a refiner and purifier of silver" allowing the discomfort to continue until He sees His image reflected in the molten mass. Value your sufferings. Get all intended good from them. They "unself" you, thus to be a helper of others.

The Inner Secret of Christ-likeness. Chapter two opens with recurring reference to the "mind" (4 times in 4 verses). This is Paul's approach to the pattern-life lived by our Lord. How shall we become Christlike? Not by imitating His life's outwardness but by laying hold of its inwardness—its inner mindedness. "Let this mind be in you which was also in Christ Jesus." Christ's life was the expression of His mind: an "unselfed" mind, giving up all His glory; a humbleness of mind, more lowly than His fellows; a mind to suffer, even to the Cross. (Theme of Study Eleven.)

Would you be Christlike? "Work out your own salvation"—this needful salvation from self, in dependence upon Him who "is working in you both to will and to work, for His good pleasure." As God was well-pleased with His one Son, so would He be with you by an inwrought likeness to Him.

Human Nature Persistently Selfish. Here an exceedingly sad note is injected (vv.19-23). Paul is sending Timothy. Why? "I have no man like-minded…. For all seek their own, not the things which are Jesus Christ's." Out for Number One! Self-ness in the apostolic church. What of today? Are we self-minded, rather than Christ-minded?

The Making of Paul. How has Paul come to be the first Christian of all time? Chapter Three tells the story. Characterizing Christians as those who "worship God in the Spirit, rejoice in Christ Jesus, and have no confidence in the flesh," he tells how his life became Christ-centered to its utter unselfing. Loaded with self-esteem, by birth, training and attainment—"but." Pressed into that "but" is all the revolutionary experience of the Damascus road.

The vision of Christ had resulted in a total reversal of values: "What things were gains to me, I count them all but loss for Christ. All true worth is in Him; seeing Him, everything of mine is worthless. As for righteousness, I have none of my own; it is all in Him."

Oh that such a crisis experience could characterize the church of today. Would that our churches were filled with folks who have seen the Lord, a sight that would make them ashamed of self and eager to go on to "know Him, and the power of His resurrection, and the fellowship of His sufferings, becoming conformed unto His death." This meets our need: a death to self; a life to God.

Paul the Type. "You have us for an ensample." The Greek is *tupos,* type. Paul, aren't you boasting? Holding yourself up as an example? It may sound that way; but in reality it is utmost humility. Says he, "You know what I used to be, proud, boastful. But now—you see the change His grace has wrought. Would that you all had the same humbling, 'unselfing' experience of Him."

We are familiar with Old Testament types of Christ, Joseph, Moses, David. But Christ had not lived His life then. Now that we know Him and have

His Spirit, why should there not be many New Testament types of Christ? Will you be one?

Joy, Peace, Contentment. "Therefore"—what? We all know that Paul's "therefore" marks a turning from doctrine to its practical application. What is Christian duty? In terms of Philippian truth what should chiefly characterize one whom the Spirit is molding into Christ-likeness? Good behavior? No, indeed. We thrill to find the answer in the realm of the inward rather than the outward, a being rather than a doing. "Rejoice in the Lord always: and again I say, Rejoice." "Be anxious for nothing" prayerful for everything—thankful for anything—"and the peace of God, which passes all understanding, shall keep your hearts and minds through Christ Jesus." "I have learned, in whatsoever state I am, therein to be content." Love, too, is included; and when that love expresses itself in unselfish concern for others we are assured, "My God shall supply all your need according to His riches in glory by Christ Jesus." Other epistles tell us much we are to do; Philippians leaves us with the urge to be all He would have us to be. This is genuine New Testament experience. When His joy, His peace, His contented mind are wrought in us—with these, and nothing short of them, we become "a sweet savour of Christ unto God."

Phil. 4:4; 2;17, 18; 1:20, 21, 27
II Cor. 12:8-10; Acts 20:24; Heb. 5:8; Mal. 3:3
Phil. 2:5, 12, 13, 20; 3:3-9, 10, 17
Phil. 4:4, 6, 7, 11, 19; II Cor. 2:15

STUDY EIGHT

What Are We Here For?

Napkin Christians

In the popular conception a Christian is here to be and do good. Jesus' answer to our question is found in two parables: the Talents, Matt. 25:14-30; the Pounds, Luke 19:12-27. We call them the Parables of Responsibility. Stated succinctly, our responsibility is to reproduce His life, to perpetuate the distinctive qualities of His life on earth.

Christians who live with any lesser aim in view, who fall into the common error of substituting a good life for this distinctive New Testament purpose in life, will discover, when Christ comes again, He comes for an accounting—as He taught in these parables. They will find that they fall into the Napkin

Christian class. Beware!

Strangely Misconstrued. Any sermon you ever heard on these parables was most likely to this effect: If you have a singing voice, a bank account, a good personality, that is your talent; use it for the Lord. What a complete perversion! Jesus, at the close of His life, as He was about to leave, "delivered unto them His goods," charging His disciples to "trade" with them, to keep them in circulation till He returns for a reckoning.

For this study, then, we take a text, combined from the two parables: He "delivered unto them His goods," saying, "Trade with them till I come."

Principle of Increase. Jesus used money as a fitting symbol of His goods since it is capable of increase by daily exchange. In the final accounting, Jesus will require, not merely the amount entrusted, but the increase. For illustration: If you loaned me $100 and after twenty years I return it intact, nothing lost, would you be pleased? No, indeed. In normal times it should double; thus you are entitled to $200. So Jesus will require not merely what he gave us, but "Mine own with interest." Hence the fate of the Napkin Christian. What if we are thus heedless, leaving His goods disused?

Jesus' Distinctive Estate. In His life Jesus created an estate with values unapproached in human history. They are not in tangible assets or material property; rather they are in terms of the heart, of life, of character. They are divine life expressed through a human channel. During this age He has chosen and empowered us to be that channel, making us responsible for meeting the need of our day with His "goods." It is the essence of the plan of redemption, first in the Man Christ Jesus, then in us, that the divine be expressed through the human.

What are these His goods entrusted to us? We turn to John 13 to 17, doubtless the most precious portion of the entire Bible. Jesus is saying farewell to His intimates. Surely here we will find the goods He left for us to keep in circulation.

His Humility. It is the institution of the Lord's Supper. Oriental custom required a basin of water at the door for the servant to wash the roadway dust from the guests' feet. But there was no servant. We hear Peter saying, "John, aren't you going to do it? Andrew, aren't you?" Not one of them would! Imagine their redness of face when Jesus took the servant's towel, girding Himself for this menial task.

This He did, "knowing He had come from God and was going to God"—in full consciousness of being God. God serves thus in a man! Then He said, "I have given you an example." I am leaving you My humility to put into daily practice. Trade with it. Would you like to be great? Be the servant of all.

Man's basic characteristic is pride. Its one antidote is Christ's humility, ministered through the human channel of lives yielded to Him. Our restlessness and discontent await this remedy.

"Humility is perfect quietness of heart. It is to have no trouble. It is never to be fretted or irritated sore or disappointed. It is to expect nothing, to wonder at nothing that is done to me. It is to be at rest when nobody praises me and when I am blamed or despised. It is to have a blessed home in the Lord, where I can go in and shut the door and kneel to my Father in secret, and am at peace as in a deep sea of calmness when all around and above is trouble" (Andrew Murray).

His Love. "A new commandment I give unto you, that ye love one another." What's new about that? "Love as I have loved you." Christ's love is the new New Testament standard and measure of loving. How we fail! We go on mere human affection, loving people if they love us, withdrawing love if there is none in return. And we call ourselves Christian?

How often do we turn to I Corinthians 13? (Read love, not charity.) If I am a man of great ability and spiritual attainment, but lack love: "I am nothing." If I make the supreme sacrifice, but haven't love: "It profits me nothing." Friend, do you believe that? Christ left His love with us to be expressed daily through us. Loving with His love is the acid test. His through-us love "never fails."

His Peace. "Peace I leave with you, My peace I give unto you. Let not your heart be troubled." Do you ever worry? Ever let your heart be troubled? When Jesus forbade it? He trusted you with His peace, His perfect, proven, unbroken peace, the world's sorest need. With this entrustment just why do you count yourself free to worry? Why ever allow yourself to take His peace out of circulation?

His Joy. "That My joy may be in you, and that your joy may be full." What a bequest! Not outward, surface happiness, but inward, abiding joy, untouched by circumstance. His joy, maintained by inward fellowship with His Father, He passes on to us through a like intimacy with Himself.

Circumstances are no excuse. Jesus, under the shadow of the Cross, the world's greatest sorrows coming upon Him, says, "My joy, My peace." Perhaps we have not suffered enough to enter into His secret. Come what may, He holds us responsible to keep His goods in circulation.

Other Bequests include His Name, His matchless Name, left with us to use in prayer, making prayer both a privilege and a responsibility. Then His victory over the world—entering into His victory makes us overcomers for our day and in our circumstances.

His Holy Spirit. "I will send Him unto you." "He shall glorify Me." This is Jesus' most valued gift, comprehensive of them all. He is leaving with us the very secret and resource of His own life. He will glorify Christ by bringing out in us the characteristics of Christ's own life, His love, His joy, His peace reproduced in us.

Napkin Christians. "Kept laid up in a napkin." What is the napkin? What is it that keeps professing Christians from attaining to Christ-likeness? What keeps His goods out of circulation? The flesh; the self-life; whatever form it takes. The flesh is the foe of the Spirit. Where self-interest of whatsoever sort has free range in the life, the Spirit cannot develop the qualities of Christ-likeness. Such a life is marked by defeat and is headed for unutterable loss. Away with the napkin!

In Business for Christ. We are to trade with "His goods." This means that He has set us up in business. Think of yourself as having opened a store on Main Street. It's Monday morning; in comes a customer. "I hear you are in business for the Lord Jesus Christ." "That's right." "Well, I'm in a bad way. A man did me a great wrong and I have bitterness in my heart; so I came to get some of His Love as the only remedy." "O brother, you came at the wrong time. Someone said such mean things about me that I let resentment get into my heart, and His Love has all disappeared from our shelves. I'm sorry. We're all out."

The next day in comes a woman, weeping. "I heard you are in business for the Lord Jesus. I've lost a boy in the war, my only boy. My heart is breaking so I'll thank you for some of His Joy." "O sister, last week our circumstances were so distressing that we became discouraged, had a spell of the blues, and His Joy all disappeared from our shelves." So sorry we can't help you. We need help ourselves."

Another morning in comes a man, his face furrowed with care. "I'm about to fail in business; I'm so worried. I came to get some of His Peace." "O brother, we're just as badly off as you are. We fell to worrying and His Peace is all gone. We haven't any for you." Like the others he, too, goes away unhelped.

Dear friend, the world's greatest need is for love, for joy, for peace. Christ alone can meet that need, and He has made you responsible to let Him do so through you.

Matt.25:14; Lk. 19:13, R.V.; John 13:1-5
John 13:12-17, 34, 35; I Cor. 13:1-3, 8
John 14:27; 15:11; 16:7, 14; Luke 19:20

STUDY NINE

Walking In The Spirit

Galatians Truth—Part II

Our last study brought us face to face with the fact of "the flesh" and the need for decisive deliverance from it if we would escape the fate of the napkin Christian and live a successful New Testament life.

The Law of Kind. The Bible opens with a striking reiteration of this law: "after its kind" occurs ten times in Genesis 1. All creation follows this law. After the fall into sin this law made all men sinners "by nature." Man's conduct merely expresses his nature. This necessitates the new Birth. In teaching it Jesus carried the law over into the new creation: "That which is born of the flesh is flesh; and that which is born of the Spirit is spirit."

"Not" to the Flesh. Christians are characterized as those who "walk not after the flesh, but after the Spirit." Christian living demands a decisive, conclusive, authoritative, and peremptory NOT administered to the flesh. No quibbling; no arguing—it is settled. "make no provision for the flesh, to fulfill the lusts thereof." The flesh is not Christian, never can be.

Delivered by the Spirit. How shall we go about making this "not" effective? It cannot be by self-effort. Self cannot defeat self. Listen! "Walk in the Spirit, and ye shall not fulfill the lust of the flesh." How simple! This is God's gracious guarantee. You do your part, trusting Him to do His part. Simply avail yourself of the resources of the Spirit, live in the realm of the Spirit rather than in the realm of your self-life, and He will offset, checkmate, nullify the cravings of the flesh.

Twofold Ministry of the Spirit. Many Christians, while knowing from God's Word that the Spirit lives in them, have no worthy idea of what He is there for. In Galatians 5:16-24, His purpose is made very clear. The Spirit is the practical, business end of the Godhead. He has a work to do. It is twofold.

Negatively, to negate, nullify, set aside the workings of the flesh. Positively, it is to develop, to bring to realization the characteristics of Christ, the qualities that make for the Christ-likeness. The one is in order to the other, its necessary precursor.

Frank Listing of the Works of the Flesh. You must read the list. And blush a bit! The whole wide range—sex sins; social sins; spiritual sins; from pettiness to murder—all that human nature is capable of. Note three things:

(1) Some we condemn, such as impurity, drunkenness; others we condone, such as jealousy, bickering and the like. But...

(2) They are all traceable to the same source, of the same essential nature.

(3) The Holy Spirit is dead set against every one of them. He detests your pet, respectable sin just as much as the most disreputable one in the catalogue.

"But." How revealing are the "but's" of Scripture. It is God's way of setting aside the old to bring in the new. Man's way is to slide and glide from the old into something a bit better. He would train and discipline the flesh; make it behave; make something respectable of it. This is pleasing to his pride:

he can do it. But—God's method is to condemn the flesh; put it out of business and introduce a new mode of living—a walking in the Spirit.

"The Fruit of the Spirit." Fruit reminds us at once of the abiding life of John 15. As we abide in Christ the Spirit produces in and through us the fruit of a Christ-flavored life. We are His chosen channels—for "love, joy, peace, longsuffering, kindness, goodness, faithfulness, meekness, self-control; against such there is no law." Of course not. Law is to control the flesh; this is the life on a higher level, a life that renders the flesh inoperative and impotent.

"Love, Joy, Peace." Here is the trilogy of graces our Lord singled out as characterizing His life and for which He made us responsible. So this is the way the Spirit magnifies Christ, by reproducing these virtues in our lives. And by these the works of the flesh are neutralized; they leave no room for the flesh. Do you ever experience a feeling of ill-will, discouragement or worry? Whence come these? Not from the Spirit: He never worries, is never discouraged. If there is ever any trace of irritation or worry, it is you, not He. You have gone back to your old way of living, depending upon yourself rather than upon Him. Return to an abiding life.

Longsuffering, Kindness, Goodness." The spirit knows how to "handle" human nature. It tends to be impatient and unkind. Here is a complete off-set to our natural tendencies. Are you ever impatient, unkind? That's the flesh. "Walk in the Spirit and you will not." Believe it and His freeing power is yours.

"Faithfulness, Meekness, Self-control." Here is the Spirit's most comprehensive work. Whatever in us is undependable, whatever tends to get out of control, the Spirit takes in hand. We are no longer what we naturally were; in us is manifest the fruit of the abiding life.

Thermostat Christians. God installed a thermostat in our bodies—a stable 98.6 degrees; any variation indicates ill-health. Now He has installed a thermostat in the inner man, the Holy Spirit. We do not flare up and get angry; we do not worry, fuss and get impatient. He controls the tendency to get "het up." He imparts the quietness, calm and confidence of the Son of God to us, thus to live as sons of God.

This Is Practical Sanctification. It is a change of disposition. We do not do what we naturally would do. Do we naturally worry? The Spirit displaces our worrying with His peace and patience. So every tendency of the self-life is set aside. Thus, too, He makes us liveable; we get along with folks and they with us.

Double Standards Must Go. Christians are guilty of a double standard. Let us divide these flesh outcroppings into two classes, condemned and condoned. E.g., murder, drunkenness, immorality; then these respectables, anger, envy, ill-will. Here, let's say, comes a man who gets drunk, yet a professing Christian. Is he a Christian? "No," you say. "If he were a Christian the Spirit would control his appetite for drink." You are quite right. Now your flesh does not crave drink—it never did; but you do get mad. Are you a Christian? "Oh, yes," you say. But, you see you are holding to a double standard when you allow the flesh its way in your life and will not allow it in the drunkard's. It is time we lived the New Testament way. "Walk in the Spirit, and you shall not fulfill the lust of the flesh."

Gen. 1;11-25; Eph. 2:3; John 3:6; Rom. 8:4; 13:14, Gal. 5:16, 5:17, 19-21, 22, 23

Married to Christ

A Life of Fellowship

Married to the most wonderful person in the world, and too busied with things to enjoy His fellowship? Unthinkable! Yet this must be our honest confession.

The Marriage Imagery conveys to us the highest conception of New Testament living. Christianity has a living Person: He is ours, and we are His. To teach our inner, vital union, Jesus turned to the vegetable world—the branch joined to the vine. For the same, plus a partnership in action, Paul takes us to the animal world—the body united inwardly to the head. Now we turn to the social world for the climactic conception of New Testament living—two persons united in marriage, to live as one.

A Person-to-Person Fellowship. What is the basic idea of marriage? Certainly not being good or doing good. Marriage is two persons giving themselves unreservedly each to the other to live together in intimate companionship. The life of each centers in the other. Each wants to please the other. Each consults to the other's tastes and desires. All this makes for an "unselfed" life.

We are "married to another." Having this Other to live for makes New Testament living essentially a fellowship. The Greek for fellowship, koinonia, means to share, to have things in common. The Christian life is Christ sharing with us—what? Himself, all that He is and has, and our sharing with Him all that we are and have. We know no interests apart from Him; He has none apart from us. This is New Testament living at its best.

Released For This Union. Romans7:4 declares that we were bound to the law as in a marriage tie. That obligation had to be broken, annulled, before we were free to enter upon this new, this wonderful married life, married to the Son of God. This is import of Romans 6: not only did Christ die for us, but we died with Him, identified with Him in death just as though it were our flesh and blood upon the Cross. Then with Him we arose, "dead unto sin, but alive unto God."

Deep teaching this, but it is basic to New Testament living. As a result, "Ye are not under the law"; the bond is broken and we are free to be "married to another." Now Christ is the law of life; we live for Him. We have supreme desire: we want to please Him.

A Life Of Separation. Married life is a separated life. At the marriage altar the bride solemnly promises: I will, "forsaking all others, cleave lovingly and loyally to him, and to him alone." Separated from all others, because separated to this one: this is of the very essence. The privileges and pleasures of married life have this price placed upon them. When separation from all others ceases, the marriage is headed for disaster. So the Bible insists on separation. We belong to Him and not to any other. Live it we must.

A Life Of Affection. Marriage is a love-bond. And love revolutionizes life. We do things, not from a sense of duty, but by the promptings of love. We want to! Think of the love that our Lover—the greatest Lover of all time—puts into His union with us. When we maintain unbroken fellowship with Him "the love of Christ constrains us"; His love draws out our love and loyalty.

(1) Love Covers. In the original, the word atone means "to cover." His atoning "love covers all sin." Again, in the original, "love covers all things." Yes, His love covered our sin, for our salvation. And now that love through us covers others' sins and frailties. Love does not peddle the faults of others; it covers them with silence. Love restrains as well as constrains.

(2) Love Separates. Does the Christian life call for separation? Love lifts it out of the realm of duty; love wants to live that way. There is no sight more beautiful than that of a maiden who has yielded her quiet reserve, as she moves among her friends, speaks a most eloquent language: "I belong to another." So the Christian.

(3) Love Perfects. His love has a glorious goal in view. He purposes to present us to Himself in a degree of perfection unmarred by "spot or wrinkle or any such thing." When we see Him face to face the sight will be transforming: "We shall be like Him, for we shall see Him as He is." What a prospect! What an incentive to be Christ-like here and now.

A Life of Devotion. All this serves to clarify the conviction that the New Testament living is meant to be far more than "being good." Life centers in a Person, in utter devotion to that Person. How often we have discovered the joy, the thrill of doing something to please the one we love. Do the same thing out of a sense of duty: the thrill is lacking. This explains why devotion to a church or a "cause" is no substitute for devotion to a Person, to our Lover; it drops us down to the realm of duty. We have taken the most lovely Person into our lives. With Paul, let us "make it our aim to be well-pleasing to Him." Let the constant cry of the heart be, "Lord what will You have me do?"

A Life Of Communion. Communion is another word for fellowship—a sharing in the highest and deepest sense. Not the sharing of things, but the sharing of one's self. Communion is an intimate sharing of the heart-life. Love is not satisfied with things—how paltry; love craves the lover himself.

Christians confess to being "too busy" for times of communion with Christ. How shameful! How it hurts Him! Hear Him in the Old Testament love story: "O my dove...let Me see thy countenance, let Me hear thy voice: for sweet is thy voice, and thy countenance is comely." To His love our voice is sweet, our face is beautiful. How can we deny Him His heart's longing for daily communion? Married to Christ, let our communion be constant, sweet and satisfying.

II Cor. 5:14; Prov. 10:12; Eph. 5:27; I John 3:2
II Cor. 5:9 R.V.; Acts 9:6; Song of Sol. 2:14

STUDY ELEVEN

Psychology of Christian Living
Philippians Truth-Part II

A Christian is a Christian by virtue of having the life of Christ. Can one live His life without having His mind? Can an un-Christian mind produce a Christian life?

Ephesians and Philippians are in sequence, and rightly. In Ephesians we are the body of Christ, the Head. Then what follows? We must have the mind that is in the Head. This is self-evident. On the human level if the body does not express the mind that is in the head there is mental unbalance. Is this the church's basic affliction? Is the Church of Christ mentally ill? Are you, possibly?

"Let this mind be in you which was also in

Christ Jesus." Could anything be conceivably more wonderful than to have the mind of Christ as one's own mind? Always kind and considerate, never selfish; always pure and sweet; never ruffled or resentful, never impatient; always understanding, cherishing love toward all—how easy to live the life out of such a mind.

Mind Determines Life. We do and say what is in our mind. Out of an unkind mind we speak unkindly. Out of a selfish mind we act selfishly. Impure thoughts beget impure deeds. It is hard to live above the level of our mind. If we had the mind of a horse, could we hope out of that mind to live the life of a man? The mind is the man. Hence to strive for a Christlike life out of an un-Christlike mind is utter folly. It spells constant frustration and assured defeat.

The Mind of Christ. The life of Christ was the expression of His mind. So lovely, so pure, it was no more lovely and pure than His mind. Simple secret is it not? Potentially we share that secret: "We have the mind of Christ." How did we get it? Born anew, His life, His mind is ours by endowment. But now, as we mature, it must become ours by development. Only thus can we acquire its qualities for life's living. Until we do, Christian living will necessarily be a constant struggle against the promptings of an un-Christlike mind.

The qualities of Christ's mind, as exhibited in His life, are unfolded in three most remarkable verses. A voluntary self-renunciation, giving up all He had created; then, as God-man, humbling Himself below man's level; then going willingly to an utterly undeserved death, that of the shameful Cross. Back of His Saviorhood is this threefold mind:

(1) An "Unselfed" Mind. Having all glory of God He had no thought of holding onto it. He gladly gave it all up, all that was rightfully and eternally His. Suppose you were God, enjoying all the glory and splendor of God, how long would it take you, retaining your normal self-mindedness, to give it up? You never would. Knowing your temper of mind, my friend, are you prepared to "follow Jesus"?—follow Him in such a self-renunciation? No, not until you attain to His "unselfed" mind.

(2) A Humble Mind. Being in position to demonstrate God on the human level, in terms of man's life, He humbled Himself. He walked as the "meek and lowly" one. "God resists the proud"—pride is so unlike Him, so absolutely foreign to Him. Had His own Son been characterized by pride, the Father would have resisted Him. But every step of His life expressed His humility of mind. And you are His follower?

(3) A Mind to Suffer Undeservedly. Christ came into the world minded to suffer wrongfully. If men deserved to suffer, He would take that suffering. If men deserved the wrath of God for sin, He would take that wrath upon Himself. For man's disobedience He became "obedient unto death." That's the Cross. That's the principle of the Cross, its meaning and value. Did He shrink from its shame? "But for this cause came I into the world." In suffering wrongfully, He was carrying out His life's supreme purpose.

(4) His Life Principle. But—and this is the point we miss—the Cross was simply the culmination of a life wholly and consistently motivated by this type of mind. His life made possible His death. Wholly "unselfed"—never a suggestion of self-seeking. In vain we search the records of His life for a single instance of it. Utterly humble—"meek and lowly of heart." Never resenting any wrong suffered at the hands of bigoted men. Christ lived by this principle of undeserved suffering before He died by it. He met every wrong humbly, with no thought of self, with a mind to suffer: "Who did no sin, neither was guile found in His mouth; who, when He was reviled, reviled not again; when He suffered, He threatened not."

The Christian's Calling. Christians should realize that this principle of undeserved suffering is foundational to New Testament living. The verse preceding the above quotation gives its application to us: "For even hereunto were ye called; because Christ also suffered for us, leaving us an example that we should follow in His steps." This life of undeserved suffering is our calling. Why do we fail to follow Him in it? Only because it isn't in our mind: we haven't His mind with which to face life's wrongs. Gladly we accept the principle as expressed in His death, but not as expressed in His life. We rejoice to be saved by it, but not live by it. Shame on us.

"This Is 'Grace' with God." We are saved by grace to live in grace. Go back a bit in Peter. If, having done wrong we suffer patiently, there is nothing Christian in that; it's our desert. But if we suffer patiently for our well-doing, "this is acceptable with God." This is Christian-suffering undeservedly. Now we are accepting our calling, fitting into the pattern of true New Testament living.

But how, life being what it is, can we attain to such a standard? Christ did because it was His mind; His life consistently expressed His mind. So Peter brings us to His secret: "Forasmuch then as Christ has suffered for us in the flesh, arm yourselves likewise with the same mind." How very simple! Don't wait till someone says or does that mean thing which you would naturally resent. Right now, down on your knees if need be, gain the mind of Christ. You are a Christian, in a world of wrongs. Bear a Christian testimony. Arm yourself with His mind patiently to endure all wrong. Mentally accept the exhortation, "Take your share of suffering as a good soldier of Christ Jesus."

And now, the crowning consideration! "This is acceptable with God" in the Greek reads, "This is grace with God." That is, when we live the principle of suffering unjustly God sees in us the very quality that was in His Son our Saviour. Saved by grace, the grace of suffering wrongfully, we are found living by that same grace. So essentially a Christian is this, when the trial comes of whatever sort—it may be His sovereign dealing with us—"He gives more grace." It is thus we become "a sweet savor of

Christ unto God." We are standard-bearers for new Testament living.

Phil. 2:5; I Cor. 2:16b; Phil. 2:5-7
Matt. 11:28-30; 1 Pet. 5:5; Phil 2:8; John 18:37
I Pet. 2:21-23; I Pet. 2:19, 20; 4:1;
II Tim. 2:3 RSV; Jas. 4:6; II Cor. 2:15a

STUDY TWELVE

"Be Filled With The Spirit"
The Overflowing Life

A Neglected Command. The average Christian scarcely gives it a thought, much less regards it as a necessity. If we read, Be kind; Love your neighbors, we would acquiesce and bestir ourselves to comply. God's commands are God's enablings; and enfolded in this command is His enabling us to realize all the standards of New Testament living. Yet we brush it aside, unheeded. We will not be filled with the Spirit until we cherish a deep Spirit-inspired yearning for His fullness, yes, a settled conviction that it is for us a must.

A "Full" Life In Christ. Fullness, completeness, the desideratum of Greek thought, is now to be realized in Christ. "Ye are full in Him." Not half-and-half life, a mixture of the new with a hang-over of the old, unregenerate self. Not putting on a Christian front, the heart scarcely in it. Not self-effort; not trying to be what we should be, with much pulling the other way. Not his; but an all-out life in Christ. Christ realizing His own life in us—His loving, His thinking, His purposing, His planning, naturally in and through us, by the Spirit. This is LIFE—genuine New Testament Living.

Illustrating Fullness. Wishing to picture the life filled with the Spirit, and water being the normal Bible symbol of the Spirit, I ask you to bring me a glass of water. Here it is; but really, is that a glass of water? It is but two-thirds full of water; so, to be honest we must call it a glass of water and air. That is a picture of the average Christian—not Spirit-filled, not Spirit controlled, but a mixture of flesh and Spirit. One can't predict under a given circumstance which will control.

But now I take a pitcher and pour water into the glass until it comes to the brim. What has happened? The air is expelled; the mixture is gone; the glass is full—filled to capacity. "Be filled with the Spirit."

A **"Full Inner Life Experience.** The Holy Spirit is proposing to renovate the entire inner man. It's a complete house-cleaning, with the follow-up of a renewing, a restoring of the God-likeness. Only the Spirit of God can do this; He has made it His business for all these centuries, and He knows you through and through. Will you, my friend, give Him the full run of your house? He wants to be, may we say reverently, your Interior Decorator. Whatever He may find needful, invite Him to go to work.

The human house has three departments, or compartments; the intellectual; the volitional; the emotional or affectional. These three make up the inner man; but all have been marred by sin. He must clean them up and make them over. It is this His fullness is designed to accomplish.

(1) The Mind of the Spirit. This is the one and only antidote to "the mind of the flesh." How many among us "mind the things of the flesh." We are naturally I-minded. We should not be; but we are. Striving against it is no remedy; the mind flies back to its norm. We need a new mindedness. When the Spirit comes to His fullness He renovates with a new mind—the mind of Christ. Our thought processes are altogether different; we are mentally freed. This mind will naturally and normally "mind the things of the Spirit." Christian living becomes a joy.

(2) The Will of the Spirit. The will is the citadel of human personality. In his will man is sovereign. God endowed him with the power of choice—to his ruin in Eden. Even as a Christian he clings to his right to make decisions. How hard to say, "not my will but Thine be done." This phase of man's ruin, his self-will, only the fullness of the Spirit can remedy. He supplants self-will with a love for the will of God as "good, acceptable and perfect." How satisfying this life, complete in the will of God.

(3) The Love of the Spirit. Man's affections are perverted and perverse. They run wild. The Bible terms them "lusts of the flesh." The world fashions its appeal to these lusts; and how the Christian falls for them! The wrecks of uncontrolled, unrestored emotions! The one antidote is the fullness of the Spirit, crowding out the old, bringing in the new, through the love of God poured into our hearts. The Spirit purposes, yes, promises a complete renovation of the affections, and He will perform it.

An Instrument of Praise. The inner life, thus made over, becomes an instrument of praise and thanksgiving. The new man's emotional nature, thus restored, pours itself out in unrestrained adoration and peons of praise. This is the normal expression of being filled with the Spirit. It is thus God gets glory to Himself. You must read Ephesians 5:18-20 with this in mind. David was filled with the Spirit; he becomes a channel of praise. So also Paul. So also—yourself.

Responsive to God. The inner life, filled with the Spirit, is in full and constant accord with God. We love His ways; we delight ourselves in Him. Every pore of our being is responsive to Him. Far removed from a life of duty we find a fullness of joy in Him.

Immune to Circumstance. As the inflated balloon withstands the air pressure from without, the fullness of the Spirit renders the life resistant to circumstance. The unfilled Christian is woefully sensitive to his circumstance. Something happens—he wilts before it. Something doesn't happen-he sulks in disappointment. Just an up and down life! But let the Spirit fill us and "we are more than conquerors." Over what? Read the listing in Romans 8 of "casualties" from all of which we are rendered immune—the love of God, flooding the heart, makes us inseparably His. Nothing can come between. It is the overcoming life in the Spirit.

The Overflowing Life. From the fullness of the Spirit comes the "fruit." And what is fruit but the overflow of the branch's life?—the overplus, more than it can use on itself. With many Christians there is no fruit, simply because there is no abounding, no overflowing. Their personal problem remains unresolved. They are always looking for help. What help they find in the means of grace they use up on themselves. Nothing for others. But the fullness of the Spirit brings life to an overflow—flowing out through us in blessing to others.

Jesus said, "I came that they may have life. But He did not stop there, "and have it abundantly." That word "abundantly" is intensely interesting, from a compounded Greek word, meaning "around and above." When the glass is filled the water is "around" the brim; we keep on pouring and it is "above" and beyond—more than the glass can hold. So Jesus said of the Spirit: "He that believes on Me" —any ordinary Christian—"from within him shall flow rivers of living water."

Not just a river, but rivers! Overflowing in unconscious, untraceable blessings, some to be discovered here, others only in eternity. Born of the

Spirit, "Be filled with the Spirit."

Friend, the Holy Spirit is willing, yes, waiting to make this your own personal experience. There is just one question: Have you an eagerness to match His willingness? Do you yearn for His fullness: Do you hunger and thirst for its satisfactions? Then there is but one condition: Claim His fullness with a full surrender.

Invite Him to Take Over. Surrender to Him your mind, your way of thinking, for Him to work in you the perfect, unselfed mind of Christ. Turn over to Him your will, your natural desire to have your way, inviting Him to displace it with the perfect will of God for life's every detail. Surrender to Him your heart-life as the channel for His love, that He may pour the perfection of God's love through you. Bid Him renovate your whole inner life. Invite Him to crowd out self with the fullness of Himself.

Eph. 5;18; Col. 2:10; Rom 8:5-7
Matt. 26:30, 42; Rom. 12:2; I John 2:15-17
Eph. 5:18-20; Ps 40:8; Rom. 8:35-39
John 10:10 R.V.; 7:37, 38; Eph. 5:18

STUDY THIRTEEN

How to Abide
Practicing the Inner Life

This concluding study must sum up and make practical what has preceded. The question is: Am I practicing this wonderful life made available to me? In the Vine-and-Branch teaching Jesus gave just one word of command—Abide. All our responsibility for maintaining this inner, vital relationship to Him is compressed into this one word. To abide, continue, remain in this unbroken life union with Him—this is the simple secret of His realizing His life in us. Well assured that He will do His part, what is our part? We pause to remind ourselves that God instituted His plan of redemption by coming to live in and express Himself through a human body. Christ was "the fullness of the Godhead bodily." He has been living in human bodies ever since. Now it is our body He has chosen to live in and express Himself through. He wants our generation to see and know "the Godhead bodily." Hence our great responsibility to Abide. Consider these eight essentials to an Abiding Life, by them to prove this life both practical and workable, satisfying both to Him and to us.

Know that Christ Lives In You. "That Christ may dwell in your hearts by faith." By faith, not by feeling. Remember His word from the Glory, "if any man hear My voice and open the door (to his inner life) I will come into him." By saving faith He came in. "As many as received Him," as you receive a guest by opening the door to him. So—"he that has the Son has life." To be a Christian is to have Christ in personal possession. Think of it, a part of one's own person! This fact is basic to all New Testament living.

Cultivate the Consciousness of His Presence. "Christ lives in me." Paul knew it—knew it was a daily, practical fact. Since He is too deep down for feeling we must do much consciously to realize His presence. Talk to Him. Recall His presence during the day. Especially would we urge the forming of this habit: Never rise from your bed till you have assured yourself for the day, "Christ lives in me." Likewise, since the Holy Spirit lives in you, reflect with gratitude upon His willingness to leave His home in Glory to make His home in you. Fervently thank Him for living in you. Form the habit of talking to Him and making Him real to you for the day. Invite Him to take over.

Adjust All Your Living to His Presence. Set one aim before you: to be "well pleasing to Him." It's a new way of living. You've taken another Person into your life. Let your life revolve around Him; study how to please Him. Consider His tastes, His likes and dislikes. Allow nothing distasteful to Him. Life for you will become sweet and satisfying.

Steadfastly Refuse Every Contact Breaker. As the electrician studies the laws of electricity and meets every condition for its constant flow, eagerly eliminating everything that stops the flow, so must we learn to eliminate every least thing that would hinder the flow of Christ's life in and through us. "Severed from Me ye can do nothing." Every contact breaker must go. Little things, seemingly harmless, if they lead to fruitless lives—courageously eliminate as the price of this priceless life.

Fill Mind and Heart with His Word. "If ye abide in Me, and My words abide in you." A person's words are akin to the person himself. When I am away from my wife, by her words she comes renewedly into my life and her love encourages me. So the Christian. Open your Bible with the prayer, "Quicken Thou me according to Thy Word." Close it with the praise, "Thy Word has quickened me." His Word makes real His love to us and His presence in us. Never a day without His Word!

Live a Life of Prayer. Prayer is far more than asking, then getting things from God—that is the childhood of prayer. Prayer is the natural expression of the abiding life. Prayer is communion, as between lovers; we resort to the place of prayer because we want Him. Yet more; the indwelling Spirit longs to make intercession in us. Prayer is the out-breathing of the Abiding life.

Walk In The Spirit. The Adam-life is ever with us. But God's guarantee of deliverance is this "Walk in the Spirit, and you will not fulfill the lust of the flesh." Trust God with your flesh problem. You do the walking: the Spirit will do the handling—"you will not." Instead, out will come the fruit of a Christ-flavored life—His love, His joy, His peace, the qualities that marked His Spirit-filled life. These are the satisfying evidences as well as gratifying rewards of the Abiding life.

The act of walking implies, involves, and expresses yieldedness. As you walk you are both abiding and yielding (the combined secret of the Vine-and-branch relationship and the Head-and-body partnership).

Draw Momentarily Upon the Inliving Christ. He abides in you to be your resource, the practical resource, all-sufficient, for every moment's living, whatever your situation and whatever your need. The branch has no life in itself; neither have you. When there appear impatience, unkindness, ill-will, lack of love, of joy, of peace, these are indicators that something has gone wrong. The current is off. You are not abiding ; you are drawing upon your own self-life. Those qualities are—you. But as we abide and draw upon Him we will reproduce and perpetuate the life of Christ—His life poured through us.

We would call these the eight directives for the Abiding Life, thus to arrive at genuine, non-effort New Testament living. Should we disregard any one of these we are apt to find our spiritual life-line cut;

then we must go on our own. If we heed the laws of health and growth in other departments of life, how much more in the priceless things of the Spirit.

An Unchoked Channel. As a branch of Christ the Vine, you are merely a channel for the flow of His life. Think of yourself as such. Live as such.

> *"Channels only, blessed Master,*
> *But with all Thy wondrous power*
> *Flowing through us, Thou canst use us*
> *Every day and every hour."*

How far removed is this from trying to live a Christian life ourselves! We cannot live such a life; it is beyond our powers. Instead, we are careful to be a clear channel, cleansed, unobstructed, chosen by Him and honored by Him to be the outlet upon earth of His abundant life. Honor indeed!

Some years ago a town nestling under the Rocky Mountains drew its water supply from a lake located well up on the mountainside. One morning a housewife opened her faucet, but no water came. Others had the same experience. No water! Men climbed the mountain to examine the lake; but it was just as full as ever. Then someone suggested they examine the supply pipe. As they did so, presently they came upon a plug maliciously driven into the pipeline. That was it! Small, so very small, almost insignificant in itself, yet it held back the entire supply of the lake, abundant as it was.

Like the lake, the reservoir rich and full, God's grace is just as abundant as in the days of a Paul, a Peter and a John. Friend, do you have a plug in your life, a small something defeating His life through you? Look for it. Courageously remove it. In this way and this way only, can you live a full-orbed New Testament life, satisfying to yourself, to your neighbor, and to your God.

"ABIDE IN ME, AND I IN YOU."

Eph. 3:17; Rev. 3:20; John 1:12; I John 5:12;
Gal. 2:20; II Cor. 5:9 R.V.;
John 15:5, 7a; Ps. 119:25, 50;
Rom. 8:26, 27; Gal. 5:16, 25

STUDY SUPPLEMENT

For use in class and group study.
Questions to be answered.
Topics to be discussed.

These studies, thirteen in number, are designed for Sunday School classes—just a quarter required; for Community classes; for Christian schools desiring a course in the Spiritual Life.

We urge informal gatherings in the home, a few friends and neighbors eager for these truths and the life they envision.

Have a notebook to record the results of your study, also for topics that enlist your interest for further attention.

The studies are packed and may require added time for complete and thorough consideration.

Each study should open with prayer and, if at all possible, close with a season of prayer. These truths are to be experienced, resulting in transformed lives.

Study 1 — The Abiding Life

1. Have you read the Presentation page (3)? Comment on it.
2. Why is there teaching in the Epistles not to be found in the Gospels? John 16:12
3. What is the Gospel? Who is its Teacher? I Cor. 15:1-4; John 16:13 R. V.
4. Have you read John 15:1-5? Do it now.
5. Discuss the crisis created by Jesus' leaving His disciples.
6. Why do the Epistles never refer to us as Christ's followers?
7. Discuss "in" as used in John 10:9; in II Cor. 5:21.
8. Does Christ live in every Christian? Gal 2:20
9. List the scriptures that teach His inliving presence.
10. Is His indwelling the test of our being a Christian? I John 5:11-12; Rom. 8:9-10.

11. Are the grapevine and its branches inseparable? (Try separating them.) What does this teach? John 10:28-29.

12. What flavor is the fruit? Of the branch? Or the vine?

13. Consider Christ's one command—John 15:4. What does it mean to "abide"? Are you abiding?

Study 2 — The Inner Life

1. What is the origin of the world's religions? Do they bring men to God? I Cor. 1:21.

2. Why is the Christian faith not one of them?

3. What is man's basic need? How is it met? John 3:3-8.

4. Can a man live up to the Sermon on the Mount?

5. Why did Jesus set such a high standard? Matt. 5:20; I Sam. 16:7.

6. Discuss Jesus' summary of the Ten Commandments as a heart condition. Matt. 22:36-40; Rom 13:8-10.

7. What is a hypocrite? Matt 6:1-2, 5, 16; 15:7-8.

8. Are there hypocrites today? Where look for

them? How do we avoid being one of them? I John 1:5-7, 9.

9. What is the New Testament's supreme provision against hypocrisy? Gal. 2:20; Phil 2:12-13; II Cor. 5:9 R.V.

10. What should it mean to have Christ formed within? What becomes of law regulation?

11. Envision the life resulting from the in-formed Christ.

Study 3 — Philosophy of the Christian Life

1. Discuss the "must" character of Romans.

2. What does it mean to be "in Adam"? "In Christ"? I Cor. 15:22.

3. How did Adam's sin affect the entire race? Rom. 3:9-12

4. Is the Identification taught in Romans the same as in John 15:1-5?

5. Show why Law cannot meet man's need. Rom. 3:19-20.

6. Consider what was involved in the Incarnation, God becoming a man after He had condemned all men. Rom 8:3; Isa. 53:3-7.

7. How does Abraham illustrate Justification by

Faith? Rom. 4:19-22; Heb. 11:17-18;
Rom. 4:23-25.

8. How does David? Rom. 4:6-8; Ps. 32;
Ps. 51:9- 10.

9. Expound God's "one man" way of dealing
with the whole human race. Rom 5:12-21.

10. Have you assurance that God sees you "in
Christ" rather than "in Adam"? What makes
you sure?

11. Explain the principle of Identification set
forth in Rom. 6:1-13.

12. Note the oft-repeated "know." Rom. 6:3, 6, 9,
etc. How do we know? Do you know?

13. How does Identification change our relationship to the Law? Rom 6:14. Christ? Rom 7:4.

14. With the "Now" of Chapter 8 consider: the
believer's new position—Rom. 8:1; his new
resources—8:2, 4, 9-10, 12-13; his new trium-
phant life-8:31-39.

Study 4-God Sees Three Men

1. Give God's threefold grouping of men:
racially; individually. I Cor. 10:32; 2:14-15;
3:1.

2. Who is the natural man? Describe him.

3. What is the natural man's basic need? John 3:3, 6.

4. Does church membership solve his problem? What can he do about it? John 3:18, 36; 5:24.

5. Who is the spiritual man? Characterize him.

6. What is essential to a spiritual life? Gal. 5:16; Eph. 4:22, 24. Suggest other means to spirituality.

7. How does one acquire Christ's mind? I Cor. 2:16b.

8. What is carnality? Gal. 5;17, 24; Mark 7:20-23.

9. Give Paul's threefold characterization of carnal Christians. I Cor. 3:1-4.

10. Can we always distinguish between the natural man and the carnal Christian? Why not? Vs. 3b.

11. What is the one foundation for Christian living?

12. What results from using the good building materials of a spiritual life? I Cor. 3:14.

13. Discuss the N.T. principle of rewards. Rev. 3:11; 22:12.

14. What one consideration does Paul appeal to as the remedy for carnality? I Cor. 3:16

15. What awaits those who use the poor building materials of a carnal life? Discuss I Cor. 3:15.

16. Name some of the adjustments needed to make the Holy Spirit really "at home" in us.

Study 5 — Saved by Grace–Live in Grace

1. Repeat from memory Eph. 2:8-9

2. Show that Faith and Works represent two different realms of life. Rom. 4:4-5; Gal. 3:2-3; Heb. 11:6

3. Explain the issue of Law and Grace, of Works and Faith in the Galatian churches. Gal. 1:6-9.

4. Why is the Christian not under law? Rom. 6:14; 7:4.

5. Show the failure of Law. Rom. 3:20; 8:3; Gal. 3:21-22.

6. Show that Law was temporary in God's plan —now supplanted by Grace. Rom. 10-4; Heb. 10:9; Gal 3:23-24.

7. Develop the resources of Grace as given in Galatians. Gal 2:20; 6:4.

8. Are these resources sufficient for daily practical living?

9. Consider the exhortation to "stand fast" in

Christian liberty. Gal 5:1. Do many fail so to stand?

10. What is falling (away) from Grace? Gal. 5:4. Refute the popular, erroneous conception of it.

11. How do you explain Paul's warning, "Christ will profit you nothing"? Gal. 5:1, 4.

12. Give your conception of Living in Grace.

Study 6 — Christ is the Only Answer

1. Why is Ephesians the pinnacle of N.T. truth? Eph. 1:3

2. Why must we learn to live the Ephesians way?

3. Show how Head-and-body teaching is related to Vine-and-branch teaching. How is the one an advance on the other?

4. Read carefully Eph. 1:3-14, as one long sentence. Note the closely linked work of Father, Son and Holy Spirit.

5. Note the word "glory" in Eph. 1:6, 12, 14. Is this our chief responsibility? John 17:4; I Cor. 6:19-20.

6. What is the Church? Eph. 1:22-23. How does

the organization differ from the organism? Acts 20:17.

7. How does Eph. 2:1-3 throw light on the condition of the world in our day? II Tim. 3:1-7, 13.

8. What did Satan accomplish in the fall of man? Gen. 3. How does redemption solve this problem?

9. How does the Head -and-body relationship restore God's control in and over man? Eph. 2;10.

10. Envision the result for a warring world if all mankind accepted Calvary. Eph. 2:14-16.

11. Consider the Church as the N.T. temple of God's presence. Eph. 3 with I Cor. 3:16, etc.

12. Does this mean that each true member of His Church is indwelt by the Godhead? Eph. 3:16-19; 4:6.

13. Is the "glory" of Eph. 3:21 the goal set for us in Eph. 1:3-14?

14. Look up the word "walk"—Eph. 4:1, 17; 5:2, 8, 15. Why is "walk" the normal expression of Ephesians truth? (Cp. The Tabernacle walking through the wilderness.)

15. Think through the Christian life as a walk, our feet completely controlled by the Head.

Study 7 — "The Unselfed" Life

1. Note "joy" and "rejoice" throughout Philippians. (*We suggest you mark them as you read the book.*)
2. Mark and memorize the key verse—4:4.
3. How do you explain such an unusual note coming from a Roman prison? Would you be rejoicing?
4. Why do we suffer? Consider Paul's sufferings as his spiritual secret. Read II Cor. 6:4-10; 12:8-10.
5. Mark "mind" throughout this Epistle. How far does mind determine the life? Rom. 1:28; 12:2; Eph. 4:17.
6. Does the average Christian you know have the mind of Christ? Or is it a selfish mind? Phil. 2:3-5.
7. Does Phil. 2:12-13 present God's provision for our attaining Christ's mind?
8. How nearly do we fit Paul's threefold description of a Christian? Phil. 3:3.
9. Consider the transformation wrought in Paul by his conversion. Phil. 3:4-6—"But"—3:7-9.
10. How different would the Church be if it was

made up of people with such a crisis experience?

11. What knowledge should Christians be eager for? Phil. 3:10.

12. Paul claimed to be a "type." Phil 3:17. What made him such? Are we expected to be? II Cor. 3:3.

13. What does the Philippians "therefore" call for? Phil. 4:4-13.

14. What are the essentials of a truly Christian state of mind and heart?

Study 8 — What Are We Here For?

1. Have you read Luke 19:12-27? Mark vs. 13.

2. How does the Parable of the Talents differ? Matt. 25:14. Link it with Lk. 19:13.

3. Can these parables possibly refer to one's natural gifts or talents? If not, why not?

4. Emphasize the fact here made clear that one cannot substitute a "good" life for a Christian life.

5. What do you understand by the "interest," the increase Christ will demand at His coming? Have you it?

(Assign the following as topics)

6. Our responsibility to keep in circulation—

   (1) His Humility. John 13:1-17; Vs. 15.

   (2) His Love. John 13:34-35.

   (3) His Peace. John 14:27.

   (4) His Joy. John 15:11.

7. Our responsibility to use in prayer

   (5) His Name. John 16:23-24.

8. Our responsibility to make proof of

   (6) His Victory. John 16:33.

9. As our greatest responsibility and secret

   (7) His Holy Spirit. John 16:7, 13.

10. Why is the one called a "wicked" servant? What is the "napkin" that kept his Lord's goods concealed?

11. Are we in danger of being found Napkin Christians?

12. Do these parables teach that Christians are called to reproduce and perpetuate the life of Christ?

13. Think of yourself as a businessman, responsible to Christ for meeting man's basic needs.

Study 9 — Walking in the Spirit

1. Explain how the Law of Kind necessitates a rebirth. Do today's trends corroborate this need? John 3:6.

2. By the same law can one consider his "flesh" Christian? Rom. 7:18-21; 13:14; Gal. 5:17.

3. How does the Holy Spirit seek to solve our flesh problem? Rom. 8:4; Gal. 5:16-17; "But" in vs. 22.

4. Compare Jesus' list of the workings of the flesh with Paul's. Mk 7:21-23; Gal. 5:19-21 (in a modern translation if possible).

5. What works of the flesh is the Holy Spirit opposed to and why? Gal. 5:17; Rom 8:4-8; Eph. 4:30-32.

6. Discuss the force of "but" as used in Scripture. E.g. I Pet. 1:18-19; John 1:12; Rom. 8:4; Gal. 5:19-23.

7. What is the fruit of the Spirit? Why "fruit: rather than "fruits"? Cp. John 15:1-5; 16:14; Rom. 13:14.

8. Discuss each of the nine qualities of the fruit as the essentials of Christian character. Rom. 13:14.

(Assign these nine as topics in advance)

9. What results may a Christian expect from constantly living under thermostatic control?

10. Consider the faithfulness of the Spirit enabling us to keep Christ's "goods" in circulation.

11. Discuss at length the double standard resulting from Christians condemning certain workings of the flesh while condoning others.

Study 10 — Married to Christ

1. How does the marriage relationship convey the same teaching as the Vine-and-branch? The Head-and-body?

2. What deeper teaching is in the Bridegroom-and-bride relationship? Rom. 7:4; Song of Sol. 2:16.

3. Why did we need to be freed for this marriage union with Christ? How was it accomplished? Rom. 6:1-14.

4. Does failure to live as freed from the law defeat the purpose of our union with Christ? Gal. 5:14.

5. Enlarge upon Separation as the basic princi-

ple of wedded life; of the Christian life. Eph. 5;31-32.

6. Consider the wreckage where Separation has ceased to be: in social life; in Christian living. Jas. 4:4.

7. Picture the motivating power of love: in human relationships; in Christian living. I Cor. 13; II Cor. 5:14-15.

8. How does love "cover"? Comment on these scriptures: Prov. 10:12; I Cor. 13:7; Jas. 5:20.

9. What makes Separation natural and normal, requiring no compulsion? What makes it forced and formal?

10. What goal has Christ's love set for itself? Eph. 5:27; Rev. 19:7-8; Eph. 2:7.

11. Portray love as the motivation of life rather than sense of duty. John 14:15, 21, 23; Rom. 13:8-10.

12. Comment on the Christian life as a fellowship, hence a priceless privilege. I John 1:3- 4, 7.

13. Do many Christians seemingly fail of this fellowship? What is their loss? What is the remedy?

Study 11 — Psychology of Christian Living

1. Have you noted the occurrences of "mind" in Philippians? Mark them in your Bible?
2. Explain the "head" and "mind" connection that places Philippians in sequence with the Ephesians.
3. Comment on life as the expression of the mind. Can one live above the level of his thinking? Prov. 23:7.
4. In what sense do Christians have the mind of Christ?
5. In what sense do we need to acquire His mind? Cp. I Cor. 2:16 with Phil. 2:5.
6. Give threefold analysis of the mind of Christ as delineated in Phil. 2:5-8
7. Did Jesus exhibit these qualities in His earthly life? Cite instances from the Gospels.
8. Rated by the "mind" standard, how far short of Christ-likeness do we come? In which quality do we fail most?
9. Did Christ come minded to suffer undeservedly in life as well as death? I Pet. 2:22-23; Isa. 50:5-9.
10. Should Christians adopt this as a basic

Christian principle? I Pet. 2:21; 3;9-14;
Matt. 5:10-12, 38-48.

11. Can one hope to live thus except as he has a mind so to live? I Pet. 4:1, 16-19.

12. Dwell on the gratification such Christ-likeness is to our Father. II Cor. 2:14-16; I Pet. 2:19-20.

Study 12 — "Be Filled with the Spirit"

1. Are Christians failing to take this seriously?

2. Comment on the water and air illustration. Does it portray the failure of mixed, half-and-half living?

3. Give scriptures showing our need of the Spirit's house-cleaning. Jer. 17:9; Rom. 7:18, 25; 8:4-8, 12, 13, etc.

4. Name the three phases of man's inner self. Are all polluted by sin? What is meant by "total depravity"?

5. Why does our mind need the Spirit's renovating? Rom. 8:5; 12:1-2.

6. Why does our will need to be supplanted by His perfect will? Heb. 10:7; Acts 9:6; Phil. 2:12, 13.

7. Can one attain the love-life required by John 13:34-35; I Cor. 13 without being filled with the Spirit?

8. What is the normal expression of the life that is filled with the Spirit? Eph. 5:18-21.

9. Note: the wife-husband relationship is for demonstrating the Spirit's fullness in the home. Eph. 5:22-33.

10. What new place will God take in the life when Spirit-filled? I Cor. 10:31, 15:58; II Cor. 9:8; Col. 1:10-12.

11. Is this the cure for the common fault of being so sensitive to one's circumstances? Rom. 8:32-39.

12. What is fruit? Is it the product of the Spirit in His fullness? Gal. 5:22-23 with John 15:1-5.

13. Do you yearn for the overflowing life resulting from the Spirit's fullness? Consider John 10:10; 7:38-39.

Study 13 — How to Abide

1. Do you realize how largely New Testament Living is conditioned upon Abiding?
(*12 times in I John.*)

2-9. Assign the "eight essentials" as topics to be presented and discussed in class.

10. Let someone, preferably the teacher, present the Christian life as an Unchoked Channel.

Tools for Bible Study

1. A good, clear-typed reference Bible.
2. An adequate Concordance.
3. Halley's Bible Handbook.
4. A notebook always at hand.

55946946R00065

Made in the USA
Columbia, SC
19 April 2019